Growing Up with a Bucket Full of Happiness:
Three Rules for a Happier Life

By Carol McCloud • Illustrated by Penny Weber

Ferne Press

Growing Up with a Bucket Full of Happiness:
Three Rules for a Happier Life
Copyright © 2011 by Bucket Fillers, Inc.
Second printing 2011
Illustrations by Penny Weber
Illustrations created with acrylic paint,
colored pencils, and markers.
Printed in the United States on recycled paper.

Summary: The concepts of an invisible bucket, dipper, and lid encourage kind and considerate behavior, discourage poor behavior, and teach resilience, courage, and compassion.

Library of Congress Cataloging-in-Publication Data
McCloud, Carol
Growing Up with a Bucket Full of Happiness: Three Rules for a
Happier Life/Carol McCloud – First Edition

ISBN-13: 978-1-933916-57-6
1. Juvenile non-fiction. 2. Self-esteem. 3. Self-confidence.
 4. Interpersonal relationships.
I. McCloud, Carol II. Growing Up with a Bucket Full of Happiness:
Three Rules for a Happier Life
Library of Congress Control Number: 2010939766

To download the daily questions, go to www.bucketfillers101.com.

FERNE PRESS

Ferne Press is an imprint of Nelson Publishing & Marketing
366 Welch Road, Northville, MI 48167
www.nelsonpublishingandmarketing.com
(248) 735-0418

I dedicate this book to all parents who do the daily, often unappreciated work of raising their children to be caring and responsible adults, as did my own parents, Don and Marie Walsh.

The source of much of our happiness is found in being a caring and responsible person.

Carol McCloud

www.bucketfillers101.com

Winner of Ten Awards!

2010 - DIY Book Festival, Honorable Mention
(Young Adult)

2010 - London Book Festival, Honorable Mention
(Teenage)

2010 - New England Book Festival, Honorable Mention
(Young Adult/Teenage)

2010 - Los Angeles Book Festival, Honorable Mention
(Young Adult)

2011 - Mom's Choice Award, Gold Recipient
Juvenile Level 2 Books
(Inspirational/Motivational)

2011 - NABE Pinnacle Book Achievement Award
(Best Books, Children's Interest)

2011 - Purple Dragonfly Book Award, Grand Prize
(Children's)

2011 - Purple Dragonfly Book Award, First Place
(Charity/Making a Difference)

2011 - Purple Dragonfly Book Award, First Place
(School Issues)

2011 - Young Voices Foundation Award, Gold Recipient
Juvenile Young Adult
(Non-Fiction)

Contents

Chapter Four: Rule Three: Use Your Lid.................. 39

Chapter Five: Use Your Lid for Others.................... 55

Chapter

1

Your Invisible Bucket

Do you know that you have an invisible bucket? Everyone has one. Invisible doesn't mean it's not real; it just means you can't see it. You can't see a lot of important things, like the air you breathe and the law of gravity, but they still exist. Your bucket is one of the most important parts of you. You need to know about your bucket so you can take care of it. That's what this book is all about.

Your bucket is important because it has an important job. It holds all of your good thoughts and happy feelings. You need a full bucket to feel good about yourself. What about right at this moment? Do you feel happy, friendly, or excited? Do you think of yourself as a good person? This means your bucket is filled. Or do you feel sad, angry, or lonely? This means your bucket is not filled.

I wrote this book because I want you and everyone else to have a bucket that's filled and a life that's full of joy. You can have a wonderfully good life if you learn about your bucket, understand how it works, and master three very important rules to live by. In this book, you will learn how you fill buckets, how you empty them, and how you protect what's in them. Some ideas are fun. Some require hard work. All of them are important.

Once you learn the rules, you will need practice. It's one thing to know about something; it's another thing to get good at it. Without practice, I can't guarantee that you'll have a full bucket. However, if you practice and master these three rules, I promise that your life will be a whole lot happier.

At the end of this book, you'll find a pledge, daily questions to ask yourself, and ideas for keeping your own bucketfilling journal. I know most boys don't keep journals, but if you don't keep track of your actions on a daily basis, I don't know how you'll make progress. These daily activities will help you get on the road to being a great bucket filler and keeping your bucket filled.

Note: The stars in your bucket are your good thoughts. The hearts are happy feelings. You need lots of them to live joyfully and feel good about yourself.

Chapter

2

Rule One: Be a Bucket Filler

Be Kind

If you want to have a full bucket and a happy life, the first rule is the most important rule of all. **Rule One is "Be a Bucket Filler."** In other words, be kind. Every time you say or do something caring or thoughtful, you add good thoughts and feelings to someone's bucket. This makes you a bucket filler.

There are so many ways to be a bucket filler. You fill a bucket whenever you're friendly, responsible, or respectful. You fill a bucket when you help without being asked, do your work without being reminded, or give someone a genuine compliment. Even a simple act, like listening when someone else is talking, fills buckets.

Bucket fillers try to fill at least one bucket every day. They don't just think about what's good for them; they also consider what's good for others. Every day has unlimited opportunities to fill buckets.

The Law of Bucket Filling

Bucket filling is an unseen law, much like gravity. We feel the effects of gravity every day, but not many people can tell you exactly how it works.

The law of bucket filling is this: *When you fill someone else's bucket, you fill your own.* In fact, being a bucket filler and filling someone else's bucket is the best way to keep your own bucket filled. Now, switch it around; if you hardly ever fill buckets, your bucket will hardly ever be full.

I want you to notice something. The next time you fill someone's bucket by helping out, giving a sincere compliment, or being friendly, notice how good you feel. That's because you filled your bucket with positive feelings, too. Once you start filling buckets whenever you can, you'll quickly discover that you feel better and your bucket is filled.

There is a second part to the law of bucket filling: *The more you fill buckets, the quicker your bucket fills up.* Can your bucket ever be too full? No way. Can you ever be too happy? No way. Your bucket just overflows with happiness and spills over to others to fill their buckets, too. An overflowing bucket is the best kind of bucket to have.

Everyday Bucket Filling

Bucket filling is something you can and should do every day. Saying hello to your next-door neighbor, helping a classmate, or saying "Thank you for dinner" are great ways to fill buckets on a daily basis.

Using people's names, such as saying "Good morning, Mrs. Beck" or "Thank you, Mr. Weber," fills buckets more than not using names. I know you can think of many things you already do that fill buckets every day. The key to this is making sure you do them.

Why not start off your day by being a bucket filler? If your mom wakes you up for school and you get up right away, you're filling her bucket. (She's filling your bucket, too, by waking you up.) Another way you could fill her bucket is by setting your alarm clock and getting up on your own.

Learning to Be a Bucket Filler

For some people, filling buckets is easy. For others, it's more difficult. If you want to be a bucket filler and you're quiet or shy and don't know what to say, my advice is to start practicing. At first, you could just smile and say hello to someone you know. Smiles fill buckets.

When you feel comfortable doing that, you could keep your smile and change your greeting to "Hi, how are you?" Some people will say, "Fine"; others might say, "I'm good, how are you?" This gives you a chance to say, "I'm good, too."

Of course, you can fill buckets without saying a word. You could volunteer to take part in a food or clothing collection, clean up a park or neighborhood, or return a grocery cart to where it belongs. You could open a door for someone, pick up litter when you see it, or do something to help at home without being asked. With so many ways to fill buckets, I'm sure you will think of even more things you can do to become a great bucket filler.

Hanging Out with Bucket Fillers

Another good way to learn to be a better bucket filler is to hang out with other bucket fillers. Bucket filling is a lot like laughing; it can spread from person to person.

Bucket fillers come in all ages. If you pay attention to what bucket fillers say and do, you'll see why people like to hang with them. Plus, it's a lot more fun to hang out with other bucket fillers who help you feel good inside than with people who help you feel bad inside. You can tell the difference.

BFF = BFF

Do you know what *BFF* means? You probably said, "*Best Friends Forever*," and you're right. *BFF* also stands for something else—*Bucket Fillers Forever.* You can't be someone's best friend unless you fill their bucket by being thoughtful and treating them the way you want to be treated. It's true. Just having fun with your friends, doing activities you all enjoy, fills your bucket and fills theirs, too.

Good friends are a big part of keeping your bucket filled. Of course, to *have* a good friend, you must *be* a good friend. A good friend is someone you can trust. Good friends don't always agree with you, but they always care about you. What qualities do you think make a good friend?

You can be a BFF to your pets and fill their buckets, too, by taking care of them, playing with them, and spending time with them.

Special Acts of Kindness

A special act of kindness is another type of bucket filling that you'll do once in a while instead of every day. It's special because it's an out-of-the-ordinary good deed that makes someone else's day better. Here are a few examples: your dad pulls over to help someone with a flat tire, your grandmother pays for coffee for a stranger, or you find a wallet and return it to the person who lost it.

Whenever you go out of your way to help someone or make someone feel happier, you're doing a special act of kindness. The neat part is that you can do it for anyone, anytime, if you are alert and watchful of those around you. You don't have to do big things, just heartfelt, thoughtful things.

Here's another idea: check out the restrooms and floors in your school. Who works hard to keep them clean for you and others? A note of thanks to your custodian would be a special act of kindness. I'm sure you appreciate your clean school, so why not say, "Thanks for doing a great job of keeping our school clean." Once you do a special act of kindness, you'll discover how much fun it is and you'll notice even more ways to practice this kind of bucket filling.

Group Bucket Filling

When a whole group of people fills one person's bucket, it's called "group bucket filling," and you'll want to be a part of this kind of group. I'm sure you've heard the expression "the more the merrier." Well, it applies to group bucket filling because if lots of people fill one bucket, it will get really full, really fast. Group bucket filling is often done to help someone who is going through a difficult time or to celebrate a happy occasion or huge accomplishment.

Let's say someone in your class—we'll call him Joe—is very sad because he is moving away and has to leave all of his friends. What if everyone in your class wrote a note to Joe, told him they were sorry he was leaving, and put them all in a bucket? Then, what if, on Joe's last day of school, your class surprised him with this bucket full of notes? Do you think you would be helping Joe? I do.

You are going to fill his bucket to the top because he will know how much you all care about him. Joe can keep your notes and read them whenever he feels a little lonely. Try this the next time a classmate has to say goodbye and you'll see how group bucket filling really fills buckets.

Being Outdoors Fills Your Bucket

What do you like doing outdoors? Can you come up with a list of at least three fun activities that you enjoy when you're outside? Does it fill your bucket when you do them? Which one fills your bucket the most? Which one do you do most often? Is it even more enjoyable when you're with your family or friends? Having fun outdoors is a great way to fill your bucket.

Bucket fillers appreciate and enjoy the outdoors, and because they appreciate and enjoy it, they respect and take care of it so they can continue to enjoy its beauty. Taking care of the outdoors and leaving it better than how you found it fills many buckets. It fills the Earth's bucket, too.

Doing Your Best Fills Your Bucket

What if you're afraid to do something, like speak in front of your class, because you think you might make a mistake and someone might laugh at you? If you can face this fear and do it anyway, you will fill your own bucket. Who cares if you did it perfectly or not? You did it and you did your best. And, as you keep working at it, you'll get even better.

Caring too much about what others might say stops millions of people from being all they can be. Many people hold back from doing what needs to be done and from saying what needs to be said because they're afraid.

If you challenge yourself to do something that's new or difficult, you'll add a lot of confidence (hearts and stars) to your bucket. Is there something challenging you'd like to do but haven't done yet? Once you get your parents' approval, go for it! You'll be surprised by how much it fills your bucket when you take on a new challenge and do your best.

Filling Your Own Bucket

It's great to be surrounded by people who fill your bucket, but you can't always count on this. When your bucket needs filling the most, it usually gets filled the least. But, hey, don't worry. In addition to filling other people's buckets, you can fill your *own* bucket, too! There will be times when you will need to do this.

If you work hard on a project or do an extra-good job that you're proud of and no one else seems to notice, you can fill your own bucket. Pat yourself on the back and tell yourself, "Hey, nice work!" Afterward, you can even treat yourself to something special that fills your bucket.

After I work hard, I go out and have some fun. Filling your own bucket is important, and it's something you should do every day.

Filling Buckets Feels Good

You already know that when you fill someone else's bucket, you fill your own. Did you know that thinking back and remembering the acts of kindness you did to fill buckets will fill your bucket again? It's true. That's why we've included some questions and suggestions for making your own journal at the end of this book. It feels good to think back each day and remember whose buckets you filled, both other people's and your own.

Rule One: Be a Bucket Filler is the first and most important rule for having a full bucket and a happier life. Chapter Two has plenty of ideas for filling buckets. Try a few of these ideas right away and notice how great you feel.

Everyone is different, so everyone fills buckets in different ways. The good news is this: you get to decide how *you* like to fill buckets best.

Chapter

3

Rule Two: Don't Dip

Don't Be Mean

Now that you know about Rule One and what *to do*, Rule Two will teach you what *not to do*. **Rule Two is "Don't Dip."** In other words, try not to say or do anything rude or mean that will dip into a bucket and remove the good thoughts and feelings that are in it. While bucket filling adds good stuff to buckets, bucket dipping takes the good stuff out.

This might surprise you. Not only does everyone have an invisible bucket; everyone has an invisible dipper. Some people use their dippers a lot, others only occasionally. No one is perfect, and we all have days when we're upset or think only about what *we* want or how *we* feel.

I don't think most people want to hurt others by dipping into their buckets. But, guess what? We've all done it. If you want to grow up with a full bucket and feel good about yourself, you need to understand what bucket dipping is, why it happens, and how to avoid it.

The Law of Bucket Dipping

Here's the real scoop on dipping that most people don't know. I think of it as the law of bucket dipping: *When you dip into someone else's bucket, you dip into your own.* And, just like bucket filling, there is a second part to the law of bucket dipping. That is, *the more you dip into buckets, the emptier your bucket will become.*

There is a third and very important part to the law of bucket dipping. That is, *you're most likely to dip when your bucket is empty.* Think about it. When you're really tired or don't feel well, when things go wrong, or when someone or something dips into your bucket, you'll probably notice that it's a lot harder to be nice. Here's why: *How full or how empty our buckets are often determines how we behave.* If you know a few people who seem to dip a lot, that's a good clue that their buckets are not full.

Think about the last time someone upset you. Did you feel like being a bucket filler? I doubt it. You probably felt like dipping back. But if you dip back, does it help? No. Does it fill your bucket? No.

Does it solve the problem? No. If you dip back, you'll probably be sorry or ashamed and you could even get into trouble. Always remember this: *You're not responsible for how others treat you, only how you treat them.*

We All Dip Sometimes

Just like there are many ways to fill a bucket and make things better, there are many ways to dip into a bucket and make things worse. The truth is, everyone dips once in a while. You might be surprised by how many ways you can dip into a bucket and not even realize it's dipping. You can dip into a bucket by being careless, by reacting too quickly, by not thinking about what you say, or even by jumping to conclusions.

Sometimes it's not even *what* you say or do that dips; it's *how* you say or do it. Is it dipping when you roll your eyes and say, "I know, Dad" or "Whatever" with a sarcastic tone? Yes. Is it dipping when you put your hand on your hip, stomp your feet extra hard as you walk away, and then slam the door? Yes. Is it dipping when you lose control and yell? Yes. Being disrespectful is dipping.

Some bucket dipping is easier to recognize, such as hitting someone, scaring your brother or sister on purpose, calling people names, or taking something that doesn't belong to you. You are also bucket dipping if you throw trash out of the car window or write graffiti on school walls or other property.

How to Avoid Dipping

When you're feeling frustrated, angry, or impatient, how do you handle it? Here's something I learned over a long period of time, and you can learn it too: *Don't say or do anything when you're upset.* If you say or do something when you're upset, you'll probably dip and do a lot more harm than good.

You can avoid dipping by learning to pause, take a deep breath, calm down, and think carefully before saying a word. You might even need to say, "I'm too upset right now. Can we talk about this later?" It may take practice to avoid dipping, but you can do it.

You've probably heard the phrase, "If you don't have anything nice to say, don't say anything at all." This is good to remember because it can save you a lot of trouble.

Sincerely Apologize

It's important to know that it's okay to feel angry, but it's *not* okay to act mean. If you forget the "Don't Dip" rule and have an "oops moment" where you say or do something mean, apologize. Say "I'm sorry." We all have said or done things we wished we hadn't when we were upset.

You may need to take a break before you can say you're sorry in a way that shows you really mean it. In addition to apologizing to the person you hurt, you should also try to do better the next time.

Filling someone's bucket after you've dipped into it doesn't always fix it 100 percent. Even after you apologize, you may be leaving that person with a sad memory. It's much better to learn not to dip or say anything negative in the first place.

Talk About Your Bucket

There are going to be times when your bucket is empty and it's not your fault. Instead of keeping it to yourself, trying to figure out what's wrong on your own, or hurting yourself or others, a better idea is to find someone you can trust so you can share how you are feeling. Let this person know that your bucket is not full for whatever reason. Talk about what's bothering you so he or she can help.

We all go through difficult times, and when we do, it's important to find someone who cares and will listen to us. There are people who want to help, so don't give up on finding a bucket filler during tough times.

Accidental Dipping

Accidents do happen, and sometimes we dip by accident. Even if it's by accident, it's still dipping. What if you accidentally knocked someone down or broke something that didn't belong to you? You would probably say you were sorry, try to replace what you broke, and then be more careful the next time. And that's what you should do.

After you dip into someone's bucket, it's important that you try to fill it again by apologizing and really meaning what you say. If the other person doesn't accept your apology, give it some time. And remember, you're not responsible for other people's actions, only yours.

Thoughtless Dipping

Did you know that you could be dipping and not even know it? It happens when you're not paying attention or thinking about other people's feelings, or when you're being *thoughtless* instead of being *thoughtful*. Thoughtless dipping isn't on purpose; it's just that you didn't think about what you were doing.

For example, what if you help yourself to more than your fair share of your favorite cookies? Is that dipping? Yes it is, especially if you didn't ask first and if you don't leave enough—or any!—for anybody else. What if you're excited about having a few friends over for a party and you talk about it in front of a friend you didn't invite? That's thoughtless dipping; you probably didn't think about how that person might feel.

It's also dipping if you talk in class when your teacher is talking, leave dirty clothes or wet towels all over the house, or make lots of noise in the morning or at night, when others are sleeping. Bucket fillers apologize once they realize that they have dipped and then try to be more thoughtful.

Dipping by Neglect

Now you know that bucket dipping is something you should try not to do. However, there is another type of dipping that happens when you don't do something that you're supposed to do.

What if it's your job to feed your dog before you leave for school and you neglect to do it? What if the people in your family do something really nice for you on your birthday, but you forget all about their birthdays? What if you forget to say thank you for the gifts you received? What about that promise to help that you didn't keep?

All of these are examples of dipping by neglect because you overlooked or forgot to do something you should have done. While everyone is guilty of dipping by neglect, once you become aware of it, you'll be less likely to do it.

Selective Dipping

Selective dipping is a common practice. There are times adults do it. Brothers and sisters do it. Whole groups of people selectively dip by acting as if they are more important or better than another group.

You might think you're a terrific bucket filler because you do so many wonderful things. But what if you're choosy about the people you're nice to? What if you're only nice to a select group of friends and you're actually rude or a bully to others? You are selective dipping.

Let's say you're a super-good athlete or always get top grades in math. Does that give you the right to brag, show off, tease, and act superior to your brother, sister, or classmate who maybe isn't as great as you are at sports or math? No, because it's dipping when you act like you're better than another person.

Because selective dipping is so common, you might think it's okay and doesn't hurt. It's not okay, and it does hurt. If you want your bucket to stay filled, consider how other people feel and treat them the way you would like to be treated. Be sure to give *everyone* respect, not just a select few. You don't have to hang out with everyone, but you do have to be respectful to everyone.

Group Dipping

Group dipping is selective dipping done by a group. You've probably seen groups of people who like to hang out together and show off by making fun of others. Laughing at others and calling them names that no one would want to be called are signs of their empty buckets. People who do these things want others to think they're funny and cool.

There's nothing cool about people who hang out and make fun of others. One person dipping is bad enough. It's worse when it's two people dipping (a double dip), three people dipping (a triple dip), or four or more people dipping (a group dip). It's a lot harder to protect your bucket when more than one person is dipping into it. If you've ever been the target of a group dip, you know how much it hurts.

Here are a few things to consider before you launch or join a group dipping session:

- How do you feel when people laugh at and pick on you?

- If you don't want people to put you down, don't put them down.

- If you hang out with people who like to dip, you could begin dipping more, too. Dipping can spread, like a cold, so choose the people you hang out with carefully.

It's wonderfully bucket filling to laugh and have fun with your friends, as long as it isn't at the expense of someone else.

Dipping on Television

It wouldn't surprise me if you thought it was okay to laugh and make fun of others. Why? Because many TV programs teach us it's okay to do that. Some shows actually play recorded laughter after accidents, name-calling, and put-downs. It's hard to believe, but *they want you to laugh at bucket dipping!*

The next time you're watching TV or a video with your family or friends, think about bucket dipping. Have everyone count how many times they see people dipping into each other's buckets. You'll be surprised by how often it happens.

But no matter what you see on television or anywhere else, it's *not* okay or funny to laugh at others or put them down. In real life, bucket dipping hurts and it's not a joke. Don't copy the people on TV (or in real life!) who ridicule others. Remember, you want to fill buckets, not dip into them!

Cheating Is Dipping

If you cheat, you're dipping. I'd like you to think about how many buckets you would dip into if you decided to cheat. How about those of your family, your teacher, your classmates, and yourself? That's a lot of buckets.

Cheating is stealing and lying combined. You cheat when you copy work that belongs to someone else (that's stealing) and say it's yours (that's lying). Even if your friends let you copy their work or test answers, you'd still be lying, wouldn't you? After all, it's not your work.

People who cheat don't have full buckets because they have to hide what they're doing and they're always worried about getting caught. While it may be tempting to cheat, steal, or lie, it's never worth it. You can get into so much trouble. And once you start doing these things, just like other kinds of dipping, they can become a bad habit. My advice is, don't start. Honesty *in everything you do* will help keep your bucket full.

Name-Calling Is Dipping

Did you know that it's much easier for you to notice when other people dip than when you dip? It's true. What if you see someone dipping and you yell out, "Bucket dipper!" Aren't you dipping, too? Yes, you are. Whenever you call people names, you're dipping.

We all dip once in a while and that doesn't make us bucket dippers. Instead of labeling someone as a bucket dipper, you could just ask, "Are you bucket filling or bucket dipping right now?" Let them respond. If their reply is, "I was only kidding," that's no excuse. It's still dipping.

Even though name-calling happens just about everywhere, does that make it right? No. You just read about bucket dipping on television and in movies. What about in books? Can you think of any books you've read that indicate it's funny to call people names? You can be sure that nobody likes to be insulted any more than you do.

Disagreeing Isn't Dipping

It's common for people to see things differently and disagree. We all see things in our own way. In fact, there are at least three ways to look at things: your way, the other person's way, and the truth, which is usually somewhere in between.

Disagreeing isn't dipping unless you call people names, talk behind their backs, or act like you're always right. You're dipping when you don't show respect for someone else's views or opinions. Bucket fillers can disagree without being mean.

My advice is to listen and at least *try* to see things from the other person's point of view. When it's your turn to talk, think before you speak. Then, say what you mean, mean what you say, but don't be mean. Now, that's easy to say but not always easy to do, especially when you are upset or convinced that you are right. It helps to remember that no one is right all the time and being respectful is more important than being right. Who knows? Maybe you'll even work out an agreement that makes you both happy.

Long-Handled Dipping

You don't have to be face to face to empty someone's bucket. Some people have dippers with very long handles that can reach into a bucket from anywhere in the world. Actually, it's easier to be mean-spirited when you don't have to look directly at someone.

You're using a long-handled dipper if you gossip, spread rumors, or say horrible things to make fun of others behind their backs. Long-handled dippers also use the internet, email, or cell phones to send pictures or text messages that can dip into buckets anywhere. Once you send it, you can't take it back, you lose control of who sees it, and you become responsible for it. If you receive inappropriate messages or pictures, don't forward them, reply to them, or delete them. Get help from a trusted family member, teacher, or friend.

Just like group dipping, long-handled dipping usually hurts more than face-to-face dipping because it spreads to a lot more people and that makes it harder to protect what's in your bucket.

If It's True, Is It Dipping?

People have asked me whether they are bucket dipping when they repeat something bad, *but true*, about a person. The answer is yes and no.

It *is* dipping when it's gossip, because it hurts when people talk about you behind your back, share your secrets, or put you down. It's *not* dipping if you are repeating the story to try to understand it better, to decide how to help, or to tell people who should know what happened.

Let's say you get a bad grade, strike out, or make a mistake. Would you want everyone talking about it? No. It usually makes you feel worse. Remember **Rule Two: Don't Dip**; *If you don't have anything nice to say, don't say anything at all.*

Adults Running on Empty

Did you know that your parents, teachers, and other adults have buckets that can become emptied, too? It's true. They might not even realize that their buckets are empty. When adults are very tired, worried, in a hurry, or having a bad day, their buckets are usually not full. And, because their buckets are empty, they might dip, even if they don't mean to.

Can you see why it's important to keep your bucket filled? When you're feeling good and your bucket is full, it's easy to be a bucket filler. But when you're feeling bad or on overload, it's a challenge to be a bucket filler. We are all more likely to dip when our buckets are empty.

When someone you know looks like their bucket might be low, that's a really good time to think of something you could do to fill it.

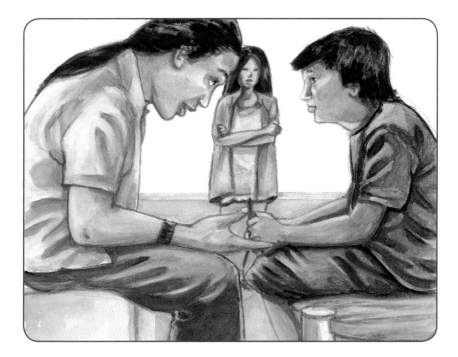

Getting Grounded Isn't Dipping

If you are grounded because you didn't do your homework, came home late, or didn't clean your room, you can't tell your parents that they are dipping into your bucket. It's a nice try, but it's not true. Actually, it was *you* who did the dipping.

Being grounded is a reasonable consequence of not doing what you were supposed to do or doing something you shouldn't have done. Consequences help us learn. Instead of complaining or blaming others, own up to it! Excuses don't usually help. Be a bucket filler. Admit you made a mistake and promise you will try to do better.

Dipping into Your Own Bucket

Why would you ever dip into your own bucket? Probably because you don't know you're doing it. You dip into your own bucket whenever you compare yourself to others and think that you're not as smart, as good-looking, or as popular as they are. While it's normal to think that others have it better than you, you dip into your own bucket when you spend too much time being jealous or envious of others.

Have you ever had thoughts or ideas like "She's better than I am" or "He has more than I do"? That's dipping into your own bucket. How do you know you're dipping? You can tell you're dipping because it hurts and you feel sad or angry when you have these thoughts.

You also dip into your own bucket when you expect yourself to be perfect. You'll be glad to know that no one is perfect; some people just think they are. Actually, we are all works in progress. If you want to be happy, watch the negative things you think and say about yourself and don't compare yourself to others. Be the best YOU, not a second-best copy of someone else, and be a bucket filler.

I have to admit, **Rule Two: Don't Dip** is easier said than done. It's hard work to pay attention to what you think, say, and do, and it takes plenty of practice not to dip when you're upset. You might have to break some bad habits. You probably won't be able to eliminate bucket dipping totally, but you can reduce it now that you can recognize it.

Remember, we all dip, but learning to put our dippers aside and not dip is a big part of keeping everyone's buckets filled, including your own.

Chapter

4

Rule Three: Use Your Lid

Protect Your Bucket

Even if you are doing a great job of following **Rule One: Be a Bucket Filler** and **Rule Two: Don't Dip,** your bucket won't stay full and you won't be happy if you don't learn and practice **Rule Three: Use Your Lid**. In other words, guard and protect the good thoughts and feelings inside your bucket with your lid.

Most people don't even know they have a lid, and if you don't know about it, you can't use it. Just like the invisible bucket and dipper, everyone has an invisible lid, and there will be times when you will need it.

Do you know that you could be the best bucket filler in the world and almost never dip, yet your bucket could still be empty? You might be wondering, "How does that happen?" Well, think about it. If you haven't learned how to stop others from dipping into your bucket, how will your bucket ever stay filled?

So, are you ready to learn about your lid and how it works? Good, read on!

"Ouch!" Means Your Bucket Is Getting Dipped

There is no denying that bucket dipping can hurt, but you don't have to let it empty your bucket. Think of your bucket as being filled with your most valuable belongings. Do you want other people to reach into your bucket and take out your things? No way!

Let's imagine this bucketdipping situation: A classmate intentionally trips you outside school. Another classmate sees it and starts to laugh. You feel that immediate "ouch," just like most people would. You might feel angry, hurt, embarrassed, or scared. Those feelings are signals that someone is getting into your bucket and you need to get out your lid.

The Law of the Lid

You've learned the laws of bucket filling and bucket dipping; now it's time to learn the law of the lid: *When someone dips into your bucket, your lid controls how much is taken out.* Your lid is the thoughtful, clear-thinking part of yourself that protects what's in your bucket. Your lid allows you to understand that when other people are uncaring or mean to anyone, they are the ones who have the problem. Either they have not learned to be bucket fillers or their buckets are not full. Unkind, insensitive, offensive behavior tells you that the person behaving this way has a problem, not you.

The very moment you stop, think, and visualize their empty buckets, and understand *why* they are dipping, you are using your lid. The reverse is also true. If you don't stop to think and understand *why* people dip, you aren't using your lid. And, if you don't use your lid, how can you control what other people take out of your bucket? You can't.

Does it feel good when someone tries to dip into your bucket? No. Even with your lid in place, you might lose a few happy thoughts and feelings. Your lid might get bumped, but your bucket won't get emptied once your lid is in place. Congratulations. You have succeeded in not letting someone else's bad behavior or unkind words empty your bucket or cause you to react poorly. Way to go!

How I Learned the Law of the Lid

I first learned about the law of the lid and *why* people dip from my mother, and you can learn it too. She didn't call it the "Law of the Lid," but that's what it is because this law protects your bucket. I wish everyone knew this law because it would keep a lot of buckets from getting emptied and keep a lot of people from feeling sad.

When I was about eleven years old, I overheard a neighbor tell my grandma that she thought I had the skinniest, ugliest legs she had ever seen. My grandma didn't know that I heard her, but—ouch!—those words hurt me deep down inside. I didn't know I had a bucket then, but I could feel something being emptied. I immediately felt bad about my legs and myself, and I felt that way for a long time. I felt so bad that I didn't want my legs to show because I thought other people would think my legs were ugly, too.

Finally, I told my mother and she talked with me and helped me. She said that the negative words other people say have more to do with them than with the person they are talking about. She also said that people who are hurting inside will often say things that can hurt others. She told me I had to learn not to listen to or believe everything everyone says or I would never be happy.

Then she hugged me and said my legs were exactly right for me. She reminded me that I was one of the fastest kids in the neighborhood. She filled my bucket and right then she taught me how to use my lid.

If I had instantly believed all the people who ever made fun of me or called me a name, my bucket would still be empty. All these years later, I still remember the remark about my skinny legs, but it no longer dips into my bucket.

It's hard to know *why* some people's buckets are empty. Maybe something happened that upset them. Maybe no one ever fills their buckets. Maybe they're going through a difficult time. Maybe they're jealous or showing off, hoping someone will laugh with them. When you think about people with empty buckets, it's not too hard to feel sorry for them. Just don't let them empty yours.

Don't Believe It!

I wonder why we believe the words of people who make fun of us and ridicule us when, the truth is, they are the ones with the empty buckets. Sadly, many people don't realize how their harsh words can hurt others and themselves, yet these comments can cause deep pain that lasts a lifetime when you choose to believe them.

You've probably heard the old phrase, "Sticks and stones may break my bones, but words will never hurt me." That's totally not true. Words can, and do, hurt. But, this is important—if you understand that not everyone is a bucket filler and dipping starts with an empty bucket, then you *can* keep your bucket filled.

When you believe the bucketdipping words that other people say about you and then repeat them yourself, you're in trouble, just like I was. I was dipping into my own bucket and not using my lid. That's breaking **Rule Two** and **Rule Three**!

Facts of Living

Protecting the positive thoughts and feelings in your bucket is not always easy, but you can do it. It will help if you're aware of some major disappointments that most people share. These ten "facts of living" will help you realize that you can't control everything. There are some situations that you must accept and then move on:

1. Some people will be your good friends, and some will not.

2. Sometimes even good friends and family will let you down. Sometimes you'll let them down, too.

3. Sometimes you'll make the team, and sometimes you won't.

4. Sometimes you'll win, and sometimes you'll lose.

5. Some people you like won't like you back.

6. Sometimes you'll work hard and get a good grade, and sometimes you'll work hard and not get a good grade.

7. Some people will judge you even before they get to know you.

8. Some people will say or do things that hurt you very much.

9. Some things in life are just not fair.

10. No one gets to choose the body or the talents they are born with, only what they do with them.

If one or more of these things happens to you, and you feel that big "ouch," put your lid on by understanding that these events happen to nearly everyone at some time in their lives. And, while they may terribly disappoint you and remove some of your good thoughts and feelings, they don't have to totally empty your bucket. With time and understanding, you'll be able to accept these disappointments and know that you are okay, you'll be okay in the future, and you will get through this.

Let Go of Bad Feelings

It's normal to feel hurt or angry when people dip into your bucket, but you can't hold onto these feelings if you want your bucket to stay filled. If you remember the "facts of living" and understand that when people dip, their buckets are usually empty, you can let go of bad feelings.

Here's a little test. Ask yourself a couple of questions: *Is there something I'm still hurt over or angry about that happened a long time ago? Have I said things like "I'll never forgive them for that" or "I still hate her"?* If you answered yes to either question, you're holding on to negative feelings, and you're dipping into your own bucket!

If you're still upset over something that happened a while ago and don't want your bucket empty, there are four important actions to take:

1. Re-read the "facts of living" list.

2. Whatever negative memory you're holding on to, let it go.

3. Forgive the person, or people, in your heart.

4. Get help if you can't do this on your own.

Learning to forgive others and replace negative feelings with positive ones is not an easy task. However, if you want your bucket to stay filled, you need to work on letting go of your unhappy feelings and forgiving others.

It helps to remember that we all have said and done things we shouldn't have. Wouldn't you want understanding and forgiveness for any dipping you might have done? Here's the good news about forgiving others and letting go of those feelings: you *can* do it, and when you do, you get the positive thoughts and feelings back in your bucket.

How to Deal with Dipping

I wish bucket dipping would never, ever happen, but it does happen every day all over the world. So, in addition to understanding it, you also need to know what to do about it. When more people learn how to use their lids and deal with bucket dipping properly, there will be a lot less dipping and a lot more filled buckets.

I wish I could say that there was one simple response for every negative situation you will face, but there is no easy fix. There are many types and degrees of dipping and just as many ways to respond to them. The first and most important response is to understand that *the person who is dipping has the problem.*

Let's review what you've learned so far. Let's say that someone at school says or does something rude. It could be a major or a minor dip. The first thing to do is to stop, think, and consider what that person might be experiencing. That's good, because you just put your lid on your bucket. Now that your lid is on, can you think of some good choices for what to do next? Here are some ideas for you:

- You could choose to ignore what happened and just let it go. (If you say or do something back, you could make the situation worse.) Remember, it's their bucket that's empty.

- You could act surprised, use humor, or ask a question. For example, "I can't believe you would cut in front of others" or "Did you know the end of the line is back there?"

- You could ask the person to stop or you could say, "I don't like it when you call me that name. Please don't do it again."

- You could walk away, perhaps with a friend, until things get better.

- You could ask the person who is upset or angry, "What's wrong?" or "What's bothering you?"

- You could talk with someone who will help you figure out what to do.

- If you can't get the person or people to stop dipping, or if you feel sad or scared, leave and get help right away.

- Always, always go to a person you trust right away if you don't feel safe, if you're being threatened with harm, or if you're being hurt in any way.

Now that you know what you *can* do when you're around someone being rude, here are some things you should *not* do if you want your bucket to stay filled:

- You should not take it personally by thinking something is wrong with you. (That's both dipping into your own bucket and not using your lid.)

- You should not dip back by trying to hurt them. (That's dipping into the other person's bucket and your own.)

Rule Three: Use Your Lid starts by learning to stop, think, and understand what's happening, and then deciding what to do next. It's not easy to know when to ignore something or when to speak up. Different things work at different times and in different situations. If the dipping continues though, don't ignore it; get help and talk to someone you trust.

Your Lid Is Temporary

Things are bound to happen that will dip into your bucket because the world isn't perfect and people aren't perfect either. That's why you need your lid. However, it's important to know that your lid is meant to be *short-term* or *temporary* protection for your bucket. Don't keep it on all the time.

For example, don't be afraid to make friends just because one friend let you down. Don't stop trying out for the team just because you failed on your first few attempts.

If your lid is always on your bucket, how will your bucket ever get filled? It won't! You should use your lid only when you feel your bucket starting to get dipped. Once you know you have a lid, you can always grab it and use it if you need to.

With practice, time, and help from others, you *can* master **Rule Three: Use Your Lid**. For most of us, **Rule Three** is the most difficult to learn.

Sometimes even adults don't grab their lids and put them on their buckets when they should. Instead of stopping to think, they dip back or let people they don't even know (like other drivers on the road who cut in front of them) empty their buckets. So it doesn't matter how old we are, we can all learn to protect the happy thoughts and feelings in our buckets. How? By using our lids!

When we learn to use our lids to protect our buckets (**Rule Three**) and don't dip back (**Rule Two**), our buckets stay full! Promise yourself that you will not give up on practicing this rule, no matter how hard it gets. You *can* protect the good stuff in your bucket, and you *can* keep it filled.

Chapter 5

Use Your Lid for Others

Protect Other People's Buckets

So far you've learned how to fill buckets, recognize and avoid dipping, and protect what's in your bucket by using your lid. Now, it's time to learn the second part of **Rule Three: Use Your Lid.** The second part is this: *You can also use your lid to protect the treasure in other people's buckets.*

55

What if you see someone being bullied and getting his or her bucket dipped? You have an important choice to make.

- Would you *stand by* and do nothing? Doing nothing is a choice.

- Would you encourage or join the person who is dipping or bullying?

- Or, would you use your lid and *stand up* for the person who is being hurt?

You'd be amazed by how much it fills someone's bucket when you stand up for them. You'd also be amazed by how often the bucket dipping, or bullying, will stop when someone steps up, stands up, and speaks up.

However, if you don't feel safe speaking to the person who is doing the bullying, get others to help or tell an adult right away. Whether you decide to step in or not, be sure to come to the aid of the person whose bucket was being dipped. That's using your lid to help someone else and that's being a bucket filler.

What Would a Bucket Filler Do?

Let's try another situation. Imagine two girls on school property who are threatening to hurt another girl, named Maya, who is alone. You hear what the two girls are saying, and it's not very nice. Maya's bucket is getting dipped, isn't it? In fact, it's getting *double dipped*.

How can you help? As a bucket filler, you have several excellent choices.

- You, alone or with a friend, could walk over to the two girls and politely ask them to stop.

- You, alone or with a friend, could go to Maya, stay with her, and let her know that she has friends.

- You, alone or with a friend, could tell a teacher or other adult what you saw and heard. Telling is not tattling. Telling is when you want to help someone to solve the problem he or she is facing. Tattling is done to get others into trouble.

- Once again, if you don't feel safe or if the dipping continues, get help right away.

Do you know how many people you would help if you chose to respectfully use your lid to remind others that dipping is not allowed? Lots!

- You help the person whose bucket was dipped because standing up shows you care.

- You help the person or people who did the dipping when you respectfully remind them of the rules.

- You help your other friends by teaching them how they can use their lids to assist others.

- You help yourself because you can be proud that you used your lid to protect someone else.

- You help your school and neighborhood become safer places where everyone can grow up with a full bucket.

You help a lot of people when you respectfully use your lid for others.

Advanced Bucket Fillers

Now that you've studied and learned the first three rules for keeping everyone's bucket filled, it's time to put them together and learn about *advanced bucket filling*. Advanced bucket fillers have learned how to be kind even when others are unkind or unfair to them. At the same time, advanced bucket fillers aren't offended by the behavior of another person.

Once again, the secret to being nice to someone who isn't very nice to you is to stop and think about that person. Do you think their bucket might be partially empty? Are they upset about something right now? Are they jealous of you? Can you think of a few positive qualities this person may have? Answering these questions will help you understand and overcome some of your negative thoughts and feelings so you *can* be kind even when someone is not very kind or fair to you.

Advanced bucket fillers look for the good stuff in people and overlook the not-so-good stuff. Advanced bucket fillers treat people with respect, regardless of how they are treated. And because of that, advanced bucket fillers usually have overflowing buckets.

At first, advanced bucket filling is not easy, but it's a great skill to develop. It's almost always what everyone needs most: someone kind who will fill our buckets even when we don't seem to deserve it.

Everyone Is Special

What a boring world it would be if everyone looked the same, dressed the same, and lived in the same kind of house. It would also be so dull if everyone had the same talents and abilities. Life is interesting and exciting *because* everyone is uniquely different from everyone else. Our differences are what make life so wonderful. Yet, differences can also make life painful if we put more or less value on people because they are different.

Life will be much happier for you once you realize that every person is special and no one is more special than anyone else. Everyone has a unique combination of gifts and talents to discover and develop, but no one has them all. You are one of a kind because there is no one else in the world exactly like you.

Are you more valuable if your skin is black, white, or in between? No. Are you more valuable if you're a boy or a girl, thick or thin, young or old, tall or small? No. Are you more valuable if you're the oldest, youngest, or only child? No. Does it matter what type of house you live in or what religion you practice? No. Are you more valuable if you're famous, rich, or wear expensive clothes? No.

It's not about our looks or the things we own. What's most important is how we treat others, and that is a choice we make every day. Everyone can choose to be a bucket filler and everyone deserves to have a bucket full of happiness.

Heroes Stand Up for Others

There are many heroes, past and present, who have courageously stood up for what is right and protected other people's buckets. I'm sure you've heard about one American hero, Dr. Martin Luther King, Jr. He believed that all people should be treated with equal respect and that no one was better than anyone else. He stood up to people who bullied others. He worked hard to protect the rights and buckets of all people when many people were not being treated equally.

It takes courage to stand up for others and protect their buckets; Dr. King did it. Dr. King was a hero because he used his lid to help others. He understood that everyone deserves to have a full bucket. He knew that stepping up, standing up, and speaking up for others are the right things to do, and he did them.

You will be a proud example too when you use your lid for others. Be a hero. Step up, stand up, and speak up to people who bully, and help protect those treasures in other people's buckets.

Chapter 6

When a Lid Doesn't Work

When Your Bucket Tips Over

Now you know how and when to use your lid for yourself and others. It's awesome when you use your lid to protect other people's happiness and your own. However, there are times in life when a lid doesn't work.

When you suffer from a disaster, tragedy, or personal loss, your bucket can tip over and your good thoughts and feelings can spill right out. People or pets you love can get sick and die. Terrible accidents can happen. People can lose their jobs and their homes. Families can split up or parents have to go away. People can make poor choices and get addicted to substances or situations that hurt them and others. These are some of the times when a lid doesn't work because it can't stop the big heartbreaks from knocking your bucket over.

What You Need Now

If you go through any of these tragedies and your bucket is empty, that's not the time for your lid. Why? Because a lid won't help you when your bucket is already empty. In fact, it will probably delay your bucket refilling.

What you need most now is comfort and help from other bucket fillers who care about you and will do their best to fill your bucket during this sad time.

Even with the support of other bucket fillers, you may think your bucket will never be full again. That's just not true, although it can be hard to imagine that you could ever feel happy again when your bucket is so empty.

But here is a wonderful truth: Every time a friend calls or comes to help, sends you a kind note, or gives you a big hug, you get a few more hearts or stars in your bucket and you start to feel better. It will take some time, but with assistance from others, eventually the hearts and stars begin to add up, your happy thoughts and feelings come back, and your bucket fills up again.

It's Hard to Lose a Bucket Filler

It is not easy when a bucket filler you love has gone away or died. You miss them and miss how they filled your bucket with a gazillion hearts and stars. You miss filling their bucket too. Life is always better when you're around bucket fillers or people who care about you.

It's been many years since my mother and my husband died and I still remember the pain. It was during those sorrow-filled times though that I realized how much I needed other bucket fillers.

Help That Lasts Forever

While I still remember my sadness when my mother and husband died, I also remember all the friends who visited, sent cards, and came to help my family and me. I loved the wonderful stories they shared with us about these two people we loved so much. They made a very unhappy time in our lives so much easier by being bucket fillers when we needed them the most. I'll remember their loving acts of kindness forever.

Yes, even with help from friends, it took some time to heal, but the sooner I got back to filling buckets again, the sooner my bucket filled back up.

Do you know what's really great? When people you know go through really bad times, you can help them by being a bucket filler when they need it the most. Because you know how good it felt when others helped you, it's going to be easier for you to know how to help others.

Can you think of anyone who is hurting or going through an unhappy period and could use some cheering up right now? If so, this is a good time to practice being a bucket filler when a lid doesn't work. Listening and letting someone know that you care can really fill a person's bucket.

Chapter

7

Time To Practice

Now you know all three rules for keeping your bucket filled and living a happier life:

1. Be a Bucket Filler

2. Don't Dip

3. Use Your Lid

You also know the three laws:

1. When you fill someone else's bucket, you fill your own.

2. When you dip into someone else's bucket, you dip into your own.

3. When someone dips into your bucket, your lid controls how much is taken out.

Knowing these important rules and laws is the first big step to living a happier life, but it's not enough. After all, it isn't what you *know* that matters; it's what you *do*. This chapter will turn your *knowing* into *doing* and it works for all ages.

Bucket Filler's Pledge

What's another word for a *pledge*? How about a *promise* or *commitment*? A pledge is giving your word that you will do something. Are promises important? Yes, they are.

If you are really serious about keeping your bucket filled, you need to make the **Bucket Filler's Pledge**. Read the pledge below and, if you think it's something you can promise to do, say it sincerely.

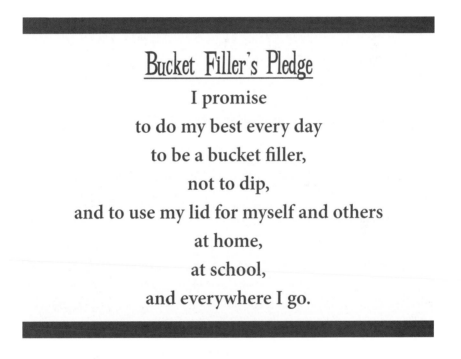

Bucket Filler's Pledge

I promise

to do my best every day

to be a bucket filler,

not to dip,

and to use my lid for myself and others

at home,

at school,

and everywhere I go.

Now that you've *said* the pledge, I want you to *write it out* on a piece of paper, sign it, date it, and post it where you can see it *every day*. How about on the bathroom mirror or refrigerator? I've been to schools where the Bucket Filler's Pledge is posted and then signed by everyone at school. Reminders will strengthen your commitment to be a bucket filler, not to dip, and to use your lid.

Daily Practice

Next, you need good, solid practice. I suggest that you do these three things *every day for at least the next thirty days*:

1. Say the Bucket Filler's Pledge.

2. Answer the Bucket Filler's Daily Questions on pages 73-75.

3. Keep a journal.

Even without the aid of a coach or an instructor, you should develop some great habits if you faithfully and honestly do these three things every day for a minimum of thirty days. The longer you practice, the better the chances that you'll be a life-long bucket filler. Like sports, music, or anything you want to do well, you need to practice over a period of time. Don't stop these daily actions until you can see that you are succeeding in keeping your bucket filled.

Ready? Set? GO!

I promised some questions and here they are. At the end of every day, get this book or your bucketfilling journal and go through the **Bucket Filler's Daily Questions**.

Here's how you do it:

First, *don't* write on the Question Pages in this book. These pages have to last a long time. Just answer the questions out loud, in your head, or on a piece of paper. You could also download and print the questionnaire from our website, *www.bucketfillers101.com*, or purchase *My Bucketfilling Journal*. Answering the daily questions will give you an idea of the progress you are making.

Second, be honest. Nobody will know how you answer these questions except for you. I want you to be super truthful. If the book says to go back and read a chapter again, go back and read that chapter again. There are many truths to learn about bucket filling, and I want you to really understand and practice this. It's okay if you have to read parts of the book over and over.

Bucket Filler's Daily Questions

1. **Did you fill someone else's bucket today by being helpful, or being thoughtful, or kind?**

   Did you say yes? Way to go! That's one more heart in your bucket.

   If you said no, jump back to Chapter Two and read it again.

2. **Did you fill your own bucket today?**

   Did I hear a yes? Good for you! That's another star in your bucket.

   A no? (Oops!) Turn to Chapter Two and give it another look.

3. **Did you say or do anything that might have dipped into someone's bucket today, or did you dip by not doing something that you were supposed to do?**

If you said no, great work! Another heart.

Did you say yes? (Another oops!) Did you apologize for dipping? If you apologized, good for you. That's a star! If you dipped and didn't apologize, check out Chapter Three.

4. **Did you dip into your own bucket today with negative thinking?**

No? That's great. One more heart.

Yes? Take a look at Chapter Three again.

5. **Did anyone or anything try to dip into your bucket today?**

If you said no, that's a good thing. Go to Question Six.

If something did happen, how did you handle it? If you stayed cool and used your lid, that's another star. If you dipped back or took it personally, re-read Chapter Four on using your lid and see if it helps.

6. **Did you see anyone else get their bucket dipped today?**

If you said no, that's another good thing. Move on to Question Seven.

If you saw someone get dipped, did you use your lid to help? If so, great job. One more heart! If you didn't help, go back and study what Chapter Five is all about.

7. **Is there anyone you know whose bucket is less than full and could really use a friend right now?**

   If you said no, that's awesome. Move on to Question Eight.

   If there is, think about what you could do, or ask your parents what they think you could do to help. Another star fills your bucket! See how full your bucket can get every day.

8. **Each day is a new day. How would you like your day to be different tomorrow?**

Keep a Personal Bucketfilling Journal

You'll need a couple of items to do this:

- A pencil or pen

- A notebook, journal (preferably), or a pile of paper.

Here's what I'd like you to do:

At the end of *every day*, write down what you did to fill buckets (even your own). Did you help out? Did you give a compliment? Did you work hard and accomplish something? Did you spend time with a friend or do something you like to do? Did you use your lid for someone else or yourself? Write down all of that good behavior. It's going to be fun to look back at what you've written and see how many buckets you've filled each day.

Just reading about how you filled buckets will fill your bucket and give you even more ideas about filling them. You can write about how you could have used your dipper but you didn't, or even about how you used your lid. Reading about those accomplishments will fill your bucket, too.

You're on Your Way

Congratulations! If you've read this book and are already practicing, you're on your way to growing up with a bucket full of happiness. In fact, the gifts that come from bucket filling will last your whole life long!

Imagine homes, schools, and neighborhoods filled with bucket fillers like you who understand everything in this book, practice bucket filling (not dipping), and always remember to use their lid. Be proud of yourself for being a bucket filler.

When all of us fill buckets today and every day, we make it possible for everyone to have a bucket full of happiness.

Now, imagine that happening all around the world!

Acknowledgments

This book is the product of the research and intelligence of others. In the 1960s, Dr. Donald O. Clifton (1924–2003) first created the "Dipper and Bucket" story that has now been passed along for decades. Dr. Clifton later went on to coauthor the #1 *New York Times* bestseller *How Full Is Your Bucket?* and was named the Father of Strengths Psychology.

In the 1970s, Dr. John E. Valusek, a well-respected advocate for the prevention of child abuse, brought the ideas of bucket filling and bucket dipping to the field of education.

While working with young children, I heard about the concept and saw how easily children grasped bucket filling. In 2005, I wondered why no one had yet taught this wonderful concept to children in a book, and I wrote *Have You Filled a Bucket Today? A Guide to Daily Happiness for Kids,* the first book in a series for children.

I am indebted to my gifted collaborative editorial and graphic team: Kim Franzen, Glenny Merillat, Marian Nelson, and Kris Yankee. They shared my passion and helped write and design a message that would appeal to preteens and teens and encourage all ages to use their individual power of choice to be daily bucket fillers.

I am thankful for my wonderful friends and family members, from age nine to sixty-five, who gave me valuable input from their perspectives: Jacob and Nicholas Yankee; Karen Wells; Dawn, Karley, Kasey, Kyle, and Matt Walsh; Caryn Piercy; Jack Padley; Jan, John, and Kelsey Merz; Leannah, Jacob, and Adrian McCloud; Kathleen Marusak; Kathy Martin; Peggy and Brooke Johncox; Donna DeWitt-Schnell; Christian, Keaton, and Jason DeWitt; Judy Byrd; Gabe and Michael Butzke; and Dakota Baker. You all helped make this a better book.

And finally, the very talented illustrator, Penny Weber, was an answer to my prayers. What I could not express in words, Penny expressed in each poignant illustration. I am awed by her artistry.

Each one of you has filled my bucket to overflowing. Thank you.

It fills my bucket even more that a significant portion of the book's proceeds is being used to spread the bucketfilling message, reduce bullying behavior, teach resiliency and courage, and increase kindness around the world. If this book, or the proceeds from it, helps one person live a happier life, we have succeeded in making the world a better place.

Carol McCloud

If you liked this book, you will also enjoy the accompanying *My Bucketfilling Journal* and other books by Carol McCloud, *Have You Filled a Bucket Today? A Guide to Daily Happiness for Kids* and *Fill a Bucket: A Guide to Daily Happiness for Young Children.*

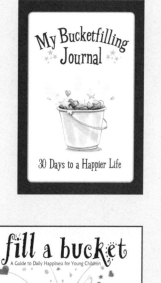

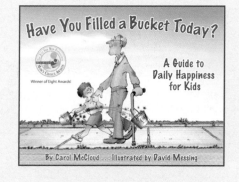

About the Author

Carol McCloud, the Bucket Lady, is the author of the award-winning bestseller *Have You Filled a Bucket Today?* and co-author of *Fill a Bucket.* As president of Bucket Fillers, Inc., she leads a dynamic team of educators who travel the world to create bucketfilling families, schools, and communities. For more information, visit www.bucketfillers101.com.

About the Illustrator

Penny Weber has illustrated for multiple publications, magazines, and children's books including *The Jungle Book, Anne of Green Gables, On My Way to School, One of Us,* and *Amazingly Wonderful Things.* Penny lives with her husband, three children, and their cat and guinea pig in Holbrook, New York. She is heavily lobbying for a puppy. For more information, visit www.pennyweberart.com.